Contents

Acknowledgements

The Publishers would like to thank Peter Cartman, an
experienced chess teacher, for his kind help and advice during
the preparation of this book and for suggesting some of the
illustrative games and positions that have been used.
The publishers wish to thank the following for the use of
their photographs: BPCC/Aldus Archives 44; Macdonald
Educational 24, 45 (foot); Mary Evans Picture Library 45
(top); Milton Bradley/RK 43; Mrs. B. Ralph Lewis 42.

Chess *for* Children

Advisory Editor
Martin J. Richardson

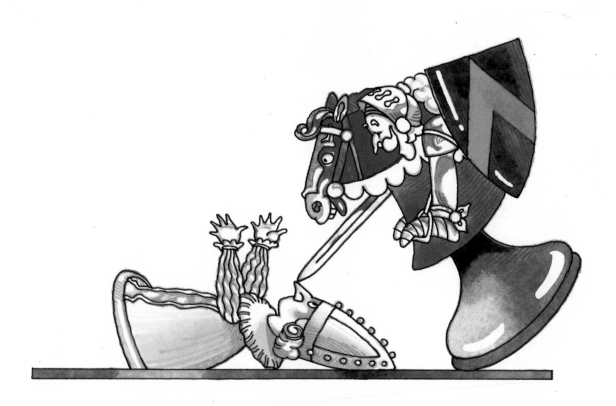

BLACK CAT

The Aim of the Game

People have always fought wars. This is a sad thing, but it is true. However, it is also true that many brave deeds have been performed in war. Great national heroes are often soldiers. Some became heroes by fighting courageously against their enemies, perhaps in hand-to-hand, or close, combat. Some carried out a clever plan or strategy to defeat the enemy. Others sacrificed their own lives to defend their leaders or help win victory for their own side.

The War Game

Because chess is a war game, you will find many features of war and battle in it. And because some of the most famous and admired soldiers lived and fought in medieval times — five or six hundred years ago — this war game uses their kind of war for its 'battles'.

In medieval times, battles were fought by knights and ordinary soldiers, and often took the form of surrounding an enemy's castle. Each side sent its forces to fight in close combat, trying to kill as many enemies as possible.

Capturing Kings

The enemy they most wanted to kill or capture was the King, the most important person on the battlefield. Kill the King, the leader of the enemy army, and all was lost. This is why the King is the most important piece on the chessboard. The whole purpose of the game is to 'capture' the King, that is to attack him and make it impossible for him to escape. This is called *checkmate*. Once this happens, then the game is over. And if it is your King that is in checkmate, then you have lost!

To prevent this happening, you have to learn to 'make war'. This means 'attacking', 'defending', 'setting traps' for your opponent and trying to 'capture' as many enemy pieces as you can. In this way, you will lessen your opponent's chances of making

war and so increase your chances of winning the game.

About this Book

This book is a complete guide for a beginner in chess. Move by move the game is explained, from the simplest detail to the skills of laying traps and snares and plotting ahead to that triumphant 'checkmate!' All you need is enthusiasm and concentration and pretty soon you'll be completely hooked and on your way to the World Championships!

In order to follow the moves and make quite sure you understand them, it is a good idea to play along with the text on your own chessboard. Ask a friend or member of your family to take the part of your opponent. If you both learn you will always have someone to play with! If you do not have a chess set of your own you will be able to buy a plastic one fairly cheaply. Wooden ones are more expensive and of course you can spend a great deal of money on a very fancy set if you wish. This will not increase your chances of winning, however, only practice and skill can do that. Chess sets come in all sizes so buy the one that suits you best. It is a good idea, however, to begin with one of the traditional 'Staunton' type because with some of the fancier sets it is sometimes difficult to recognise the pieces.

Warning Lights

A colour code has been used in the diagrams throughout this book to help you to understand the importance of some moves.

Ordinary moves are shown by green arrows.

Amber indicates a possible move *not yet* taken.

Red shows a *possible* move which could be very dangerous for the player's opponent. A dotted line in red means that a possible weakness or threat has appeared which could prove dangerous in the next move or so. Thinking ahead is vital in chess!

Where Chess Comes From

No one knows just how old the game of chess is. What we do know is that a kind of chess was played in India about 1500 years ago. The name of this game came from the language of war: it was *chaturanga*. Chaturanga meant the four 'angas' or sections of an army in India at the time: that is, elephants, horses, chariots and footsoldiers.

Travelling Chess

The game spread to Persia (modern-day Iran) in the sixth century AD, that is about 1400 years ago. After this it spread to China, Japan, Arabia and into Europe. Most probably chess spread along the trade routes which criss-crossed the great land mass of Europe and Asia. Journeys along these routes could take many months or even years. Chess is not a quick or easy game. So, it was very suitable for playing on these long journeys.

A Game for the Nobility

As the game of chess spread, it changed because different people chose different ways of playing. This is why Japanese chess or *shogi* is different from Chinese chess. Both are different from the game we call chess, which developed in Italy about 500 years ago. At first it was a game for the rich and the nobility. Only they had enough free time and the right education needed to play it.

Philidor the Chess-player

Then, two centuries ago, better education made chess popular among many more people. One famous chess player at this time was François-André Danican (1726-95) who called himself Philidor. Philidor travelled all over Europe playing chess with other enthusiasts. Sometimes he played three games at once, and he did it blindfold, so that he could not see any of the boards or the chess pieces.

Players like Philidor made the game even better known than before and, in 1851, the first International Chess Tournament was held in London. Some years after that, games were played to decide who should be the first chess champion of the world.

Today, chess is a popular game. Important chess tournaments can be seen on television. There are many chess clubs and other organisations. And some very young players —only nine or ten years old—have the chance to become chess champions.

The Chessboard & Pieces

T he chessboard, like the board used in draughts, is chequered—that is, made up of black and white squares. There are 64 squares in all. Set up your board following the picture on page 18.

The squares that go straight up and down the board are called **files**.

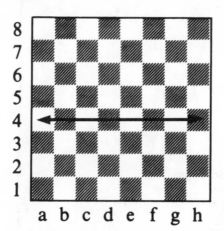

The squares that go across the board from side to side are called **ranks**.

The squares of the same colour which touch corner to corner are called **diagonals**.

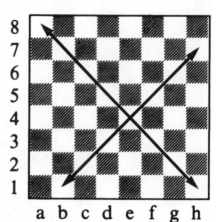

The King

As you know, in real life, a king was the most important person on the battlefield. In medieval times, he always had a ring of knights and soldiers around him, to protect him. This does not mean the king did no fighting, of course. Many kings were famous warriors, like Richard the Lionheart of England or Charlemagne —'Charles the Great'—of France. Even so, most battles were fought by footsoldiers and knights. The king was rarely there to command his troops. If he *did* fight, it was usually in the last stages of a battle.

In Chess

It's just the same with the King on the chessboard. As you can see from our picture, he stands in the middle of his forces, protected on all sides. But as you will see later, the King may come out and fight in the endgame when most of the enemy pieces have been captured. The King can move one square in any direction—forwards, backwards, sideways or diagonally.

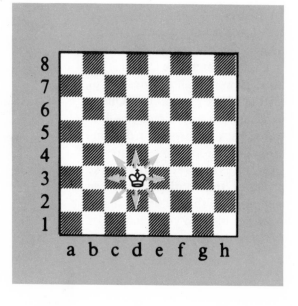

The Queen

Real-life medieval queens, like chess Queens, stood beside the king as the next most important person in the kingdom. As the king's wife, the queen was the mother of the prince or princess who was heir to the throne. Sometimes, if her oldest child became king or queen when very young, she would rule for them as a regent. Queens often came from powerful families. Many were the daughters of foreign kings, dukes or other rulers. Some queens were the daughters of noblemen. Their relatives might become important advisers to the king.

In Chess

Real medieval queens didn't usually fight in battles, of course. In chess, though, the Queen is the most powerful and aggressive of all the chess pieces. The Queen can move in any direction—forward, back, sideways or diagonally—and for as many squares as the chessboard contains, provided that nothing is in her way. To lose the Queen is usually a serious blow to your chances of winning the game.

The Bishops

Like the queen, the bishops in real medieval life did not fight in battle. All the same, as representatives of the Church, bishops were very important. The coronation of kings was a solemn religious service and it was always a bishop or archbishop who actually put the crown on the king's head during the ceremony.

So, kings normally tried to make sure that their wars—and indeed everything they did—had the blessing of the Church and its bishops.

In Chess

In chess the Bishops do fight in the battle, just as the Queen does. There are two black and two white Bishops in each chess game. They stand on either side of their Kings and Queens, protecting and supporting them, much as they did in real life all those centuries ago. The Bishops move diagonally, back or forwards for any number of squares, provided that there is nothing in the way.

The Rooks

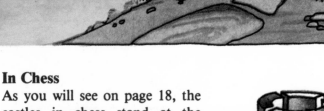

In medieval Europe, it was much safer for nobles to live in a castle if they lived in the open countryside. Some towns were like castles too: they had protective walls, with battlements. In times of trouble and danger, nobles gave protection to their retainers or workpeople, by letting them shelter within their castle walls. Battles were often fought around these great stone castles when they were besieged by the armies of rival nobles. So, castles had to be very strong and have good defences against attack.

In Chess

As you will see on page 18, the castles in chess stand at the strongpoints of the chessboard—in the corners. Chess castles are called **Rooks,** but this has nothing to do with the bird of the same name! The word 'rook' comes from an old French word 'roc' meaning 'rock' and that's what castles must be, both in real life and in chess: rocks strong enough to stand against attack. Unlike real life, though, the castles in chess move!

Rooks move straight up and down, or from side to side, for any number of squares providing that nothing is in the way.

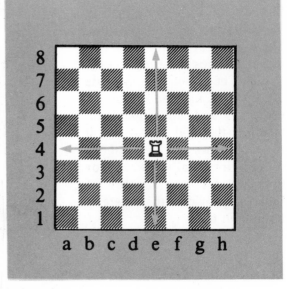

The Pawns

The nobles and knights in medieval times were like little kings on their own estates. They owned enormous areas of land and many small farms. In war, the men who worked on these estates had to fight for their lords, as the nobles were known, and in the same way the nobles were duty-bound to fight for the king. Usually men who fought as ordinary footsoldiers for their lords were aged between 16 and 60 years. These footsoldiers stood in the front line of battles and were the first to fight with the enemy.

In Chess

In the same way, the Pawns in chess stand in the front line of the armies on the chessboard. There are eight of them on each side. Usually they are the first to go into the chessboard battle. The name pawn comes from the French word 'pion' which is the French version of the Latin word 'pedonum'—and 'pedonum' meant 'footsoldier'.

Pawns can only move forward—never backwards—and, after their first move, only one square at a time. On its first move a pawn can go forward either one or two squares.

First move only

The Knights

In medieval times, it was the duty of the nobles to fight for their king when asked to do so. To become knights, the sons of noble and other important families began training at the age of seven or eight. They learned how to fight on horseback and on foot, wearing full armour. In a battle, knights had to try to move in their heavy armour as if they were not wearing it at all.

In Chess
In a real battle, a king might have hundreds of knights fighting for him. In chess, the white King and the black King have only two Knights each. Even so, these Knights are clever and agile pieces. The chess piece for a Knight, as you can see, looks like a horse. This gives a clue to an agile trick these pieces can perform: they can jump over other pieces, just like a horse jumping a fence. The Knights are the only pieces in chess which are allowed to jump in this way.

The L-shaped Jump
This is the Knight's special way of moving:

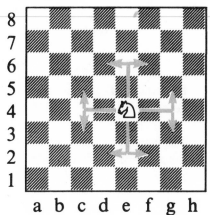

Knights move two squares back *or* forwards then one to the side—or they can move two squares to the side then one back or forwards. Like this:

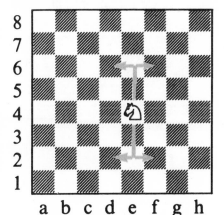

Or like this:

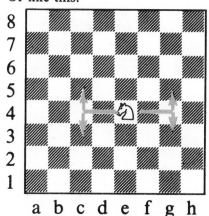

A Knight's move always takes it from a white square to a black square or from a black square to a white square.

Jumping other Pieces
A Knight can make this L-shaped move even when there is another man on the square in front or at the side of it because, as you know, the Knight can jump over other chessmen.

So, if you like, you can use a Knight for your first move in a game like this:

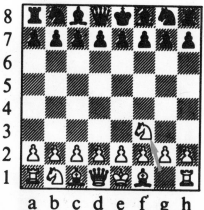

Chess Symbols

Instead of using the name of each piece every time it is moved, it is usual to show a little picture outline or symbol instead.

King	♚	The sort of crown a king would wear
Queen	♛	The sort of crown a queen would wear
Bishop	♝	A bishop's mitre or hat
Knight	♞	A horse
Castle or Rook	♜	A castle
Pawn	♟	Smaller drawing of the Pawn on the chessboard

The Happy Prisoner

In the year 1214, Count Ferrand of Flanders was defeated in battle and taken prisoner by the King of France. The usual thing at this time was for a prisoner's family to pay a ransom for his release. The French king was therefore astonished to find that Count Ferrand did not want to be released: what was more, his wife, the Countess, refused to pay a ransom for him. The reason for all this was chess. The Count hated his wife because she was a better chess player than he was, and always beat him in every game they played. The Countess, for her part, disliked her husband so much that she would never let him win.

Setting up the Chessboard

This is how your chessboard should look at the start of every game. The board should be placed so that there is a white square in the bottom right hand corner. The white pieces are always set out on this end of the board. Make sure all your pieces are on the correct squares—note especially how the two Kings and Queens face each other.

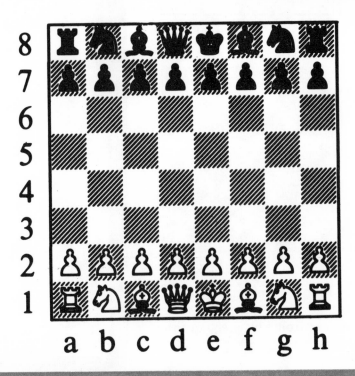

Capturing Enemies

You have already learned something about the moves of the different men. This is where you should start to use your own chessboard and men so that you can practise the moves and captures. Ask a friend to be your opponent and follow the moves.

1a

The King cannot move to the square on which the white Pawn stands, but it can move to any one of seven other squares.

1b

The King has moved! He has captured the black Pawn which has been taken from the board.

2a

The Queen has lots of moves and two of them are captures. The Queen can take the enemy Knight or Rook. She cannot capture the Bishop because the King is blocking the way.

2b

The Queen has moved! She has captured the Rook which has been taken from the board.

3b

The Bishop has moved! The black Pawn has been captured and taken from the board. If the Rook does not move out of the way now the Bishop will be able to capture it on the next move!

4b

The Rook has moved! The Knight has been captured and taken from the board.

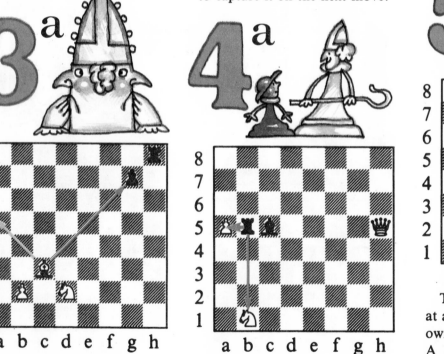

3a

The Bishop cannot move backwards because his own men are blocking both diagonals. He can still move forward on two diagonals but cannot capture the Rook because the black Pawn is blocking the way.

4a

There are six squares to which the Rook could move without making a capture. It could also capture the Knight or the Pawn. The Rook cannot capture the Queen because the Bishop is blocking the way.

5a

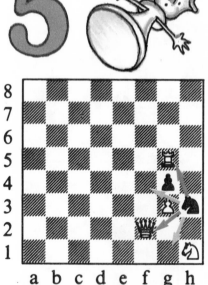

The white Knight cannot move at all until his own Queen or his own Pawn moves out of the way. A Knight can jump over other men, but he cannot land on a square where one of his own men stands. The black Knight can move to four different squares. The enemy Queen and Rook are on two of these squares and he can capture one of them.

5ᵇ

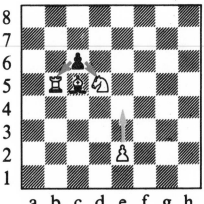

black Pawn cannot move forward at all because the Bishop is blocking its way. Pawns cannot capture enemies that are straight in front of them. Pawns capture by moving one square diagonally forward. The black Pawn can capture either the Rook or the Knight.

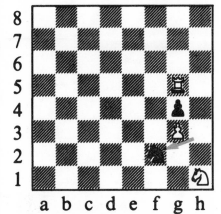

The black Knight has moved! The enemy Queen has been captured.

6ᵃ

Pawns move forward one square except on their first move, when they can move forward either one or two squares. The white Pawn is on the square where it starts the game, so it can move forward two squares. The

6ᵇ

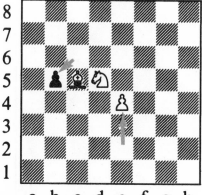

Both Pawns have moved! First of all the white Pawn went forward two squares from its starting position. The black Pawn has captured the enemy Rook.

Check and Checkmate

If your King is attacked by an enemy man, he is said to be 'in check'. The first thing that you must do is to get him out of trouble. There are three ways that this may be done:

1. Move your King so that he is no longer attacked.
2. Capture the attacking piece.
3. Put another man between the attacker and your King.

You are not allowed to make any other moves when your King is in check. If you cannot escape from check then it is the end of the game—checkmate! You will find many examples of check in the games in this book. Checkmate is shown on the next two pages.

21

A Short Game

FIVE MOVES TO CHECKMATE!

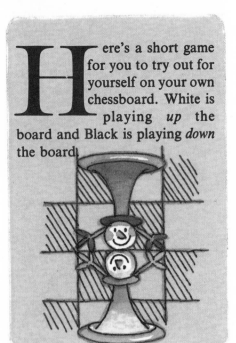

Here's a short game for you to try out for yourself on your own chessboard. White is playing *up* the board and Black is playing *down* the board.

White always plays first and, in this game, starts by moving a pawn two squares forward. **1a**

Black also moves a Pawn squares forward, as his oper move. **1**

The white army now sends its Knight into the attack. **3a**

The first casualty of the battle: the black Knight has captured the white Pawn. **3b**

Here comes the Queen- most powerful piece on chessboard. **4**

22

| | a | b | c | d | e | f | g | h |

The white Bishop moves out diagonally, that is on a slant, near the centre of the board.

2a

8								
7								
6								
5								
4								
3								
2								
1								
	a	b	c	d	e	f	g	h

The black Knight jumps over the Pawn to enter the battle.

2b

| | a | b | c | d | e | f | g | h |

The second casualty of the battle: the black Knight has captured the white Knight. White could capture the black Knight with either of the two Pawns, but there is a better move.

4b

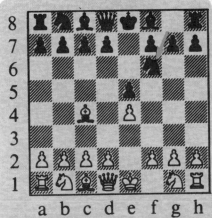

8								
7								
6								
5								
4								
3								
2								
1								
	a	b	c	d	e	f	g	h

The white Queen makes straight for the black King, capturing a Pawn on the way—and it's checkmate! White has won, even though Black has captured more men.

5a

What happened to the black King?

Why can't the black King escape? If you look at the chessboard, you'll see there are two possible moves that can be tried.

1. If the black King moved to the square in front of him he would still be attacked by the white Queen.

2. The black King cannot take the white Queen, because he would then be attacked by the white Bishop which is guarding the Queen. No other black piece can rescue him by capturing the white Queen, so the black King cannot escape.

There's only one thing the black King can do now. It's this:

This is what players do with their King when they have lost the game. The losing player places his or her King on its side to show that the King has surrendered.

Reading Moves to Play on Your Chessboard

Chess books would be very long and boring if an illustration was needed to show every move that was played. Fortunately, illustrations are not always needed because there is an easy way of writing down chess moves.

The Board

To begin with, letters and numbers are used to name every square on the board.

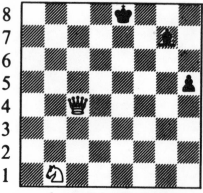

Each **file** is given a letter, starting with 'a' on White's left hand side through to 'h' on White's right hand side.

Each **rank** is given a number starting with '1' at White's end of the board through to '8' at Black's end of the board.

A square is 'named' by first finding the letter of its file and then finding the number of its rank. If you look at the illustration you will see that the Knight is on the square 'b1' and the Queen is on the square 'c4'.

Puzzler

Can you find the names of the squares on which the black men stand?

Answer

The King is on the square e8. The Bishop is on the square g7. The Pawn is on the square h5.

The Moves

A move is written down by using the symbols for the men that you have already seen in the illustrations on page 17 and the names of two squares.

♗f1-c4 means that a bishop on the square f1 moves to the square c4.

'-' means a move from one square to another.

'x' means that an enemy man has been captured, so that ♘f6xe4 means that a Knight on the square f6 has moved to capture an enemy man on the square e4. This way of writing down the moves is known as **figurine algebraic notation** —quite a mouthful for such an easy method.

Try it Out

Here are the moves of the game you played through on pages 22 and 23, written out in figurine algebraic notation. Moves on the left hand side are White's and those on the right hand side are Black's. Set up your board and men and see if you can play through the game again without looking back at the illustrations.

Move number	White's moves	Black's moves
1	♙ e2-e4	♙ e7-e5
2	♗ f1-c4	♘ g8-f6
3	♘ b1-c3	♘ f6xe4
4	♕ d1-f3	♘ e4xc3
5	♕ f3xf7 ++	

++ at the end means 'checkmate'. Have you got checkmate on your board? Compare your position with the last illustration on page 23 to see if you have played all the moves correctly.

To save space, it is not usual to include the symbol for a Pawn (♙), but to mention only the squares involved instead. In this game White's first move would be written e2-e4. So if you see a move without a symbol for a piece then it must be a Pawn that is moving.

priceless!

What each piece is worth
You can see which chess men are the most valuable from this chart:

Pawn	♙	1 point
Bishop	♗	3 points
Knight	♘	3 points
Rook	♖	5 points
Queen	♕	9 points

The King is invaluable—or priceless! Remember: lose the King and you lose the game!

Beautiful Chess Sets

The ordinary chess sets people use for playing their games are a standard pattern of simple pieces, made from wood or plastic. They were designed in 1835 and named 'Staunton' after a famous British chess player, Howard Staunton. They are easy to play with because it is easy to tell the differences between the men.

There are, however, some special ornamental chessmen which are not really meant for playing with, although you can do this of course.

From Far and Wide
One of these special sets comes from Kenya, in Africa. A carving of the tribal chief is the King. The Rooks are tall mud huts which were the traditional homes of some African tribes. Giraffes are

Intricately carved jade figures from a Chinese chess set.

The King from the Reynard the Fox chess set is a lion.

the Knights in this beautifully carved chess set, and the Pawns are the heads of tribal warriors.

The Lewis chess pieces, found by archaeologists on the Isle of Lewis in Scotland's Outer Hebrides are about 900 years old. They were carved from walrus tusks and the King, Queen and Bishop sit on thrones. So do the King and Queen in a medieval German chess set, and here the thrones are very elaborate. The King's throne has a lion carved on it. The Queen's throne has carvings of musicians and ladies-in-waiting at the royal court.

In Italy, you can find chess sets with Roman soldiers as the Pawns. The King is the Emperor of ancient Rome.

In another special chess set, made in Sri Lanka nearly 200 years ago, the Knight is a horse rearing up on its hind legs, and the Bishops and Pawns look like decorations in Buddhist temples.

There is also a Chinese chess set with the pieces carved in green jade, with gold decorations. Other sets have pieces which resemble carved statues of angels.

Figures from a modern carved chess set from Nigeria.

In Lewis Carroll's famous story *Alice Through the Looking Glass* the characters play various chess pieces and Alice herself is the white Pawn who eventually reaches the top of the board and becomes a Queen.

Stories in Chess

Chess pieces can tell a story, too. One set, now in a museum in Munich, West Germany, uses animal characters from the famous story 'Reynard the Fox'. The King is a fierce-looking lion!

Another Chinese set uses characters from an ancient Chinese legend, the Eight Immortals. Fortunately, one of the immortals was a woman, so she is used as the Queen.

27

Attacking and Defending

Real-life war is a team effort, and it always has been. You often read of magnificent deeds performed by individual soldiers in battle. However, what really wins battles is the working together of the soldiers in an army.

Think of a castle siege in medieval times. The defenders are on the battlements, with their weapons. The attackers are climbing up long ladders which they have propped up against the castle walls. Some distance away, groups of archers and cross-bowmen are firing at the castle defenders. Their arrows, of course, fly over the heads of their own men climbing the ladders and land among the enemy soldiers above.

Now, suppose the archers and crossbowmen weren't there to give the attackers this ' covering fire'. The men on the ladders would be in a very dangerous position. There would be nothing to stop the defenders pushing the ladders away and sending them crashing to the ground. Or the defenders could pour down boiling oil, or arrows, or gunfire from hand-held rifles called arquebusses—and the men on the ladders would be entirely at their mercy.

The Attack in Chess
The attack in chess works in exactly the same way. Attacking chessmen should always have 'covering fire', that is support or protection from other chessmen so that the enemy cannot easily capture them.

Suppose the chessboard battle has produced this situation:

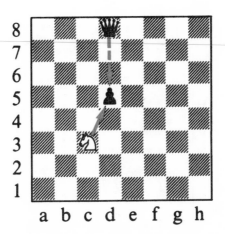

If the white Knight captures the black Pawn, then the black Queen can come straight down the file and capture the white Knight.

So, White will lose a valuable piece—a Knight worth 3 points—for the sake of a Pawn worth only 1 point. Not a good exchange for White, is it?

Team Tactics
Now see what happens if the white Knight has help and protection from another white piece.

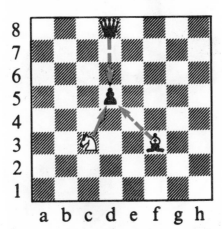

If the white Knight takes the black Pawn *now*, and the black Queen captures the Knight, then the black army will lose its most valuable chess piece. For the black Queen can then be captured by the white Bishop. So, Black will not risk the Queen in this way, and the white Knight is safe.

One Against Two
Sometimes, you get two or more pieces into a position where an enemy man can threaten both of them, like this:

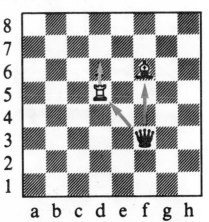

However, all is not lost for White! For the white Rook can make a good defending move. The white Rook can defend the Bishop while itself escaping from the black Queen. To do this, the Rook moves from d5 to d6. Now the Queen cannot reach the Rook and if the Queen captures the white Bishop, the white Rook will in turn capture it.

Opening Moves

As you know, the men that can make the first move in a chess game are Knights and Pawns. In the starting position, the Queen, Rooks and Bishops cannot move at all!

The purpose of the first few moves is not just to get the game started, but to open up the way for other pieces to move out onto the board.

For the first ten or twelve moves, White and Black try to move all their pieces into good, strong positions ready for the tough fighting ahead.

Look at the possibilities if White begins by moving the Pawn from e2 to e4.

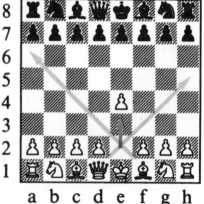

Now the white Queen and Bishop can move out across the board diagonally, where there's enough room to move about when it comes to fighting the enemy.

Developing

Let's suppose Black makes the same first move and also opens up the diagonals for the Queen and a Bishop. On the second move, White decides to 'develop' the Knight from g1 to f3. 'Developing' means bringing your important chess pieces off the back rank to where they can help with attacking and defending.

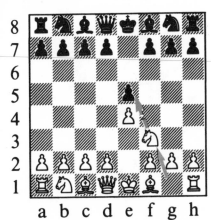

The white Knight is threatening to take the black Pawn on e5. Black decides to defend it by moving the Knight from b8 to c6. Then White moves the Bishop from f1 to b5.

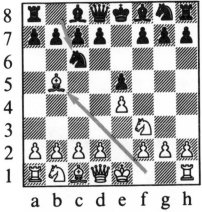

Different ways of developing the men at the start of the game have different names.

Ruy Lopez

This chess opening is called the **Ruy Lopez**. It is named after a famous Spanish chess player, Ruy Lopez de Sigura, who wrote an important book about chess more than 400 years ago. We will see more of the Ruy Lopez opening in our next game, but before we do that we'll look at a very bad way to start a game.

Fool's Mate

It is unwise at the start to move the Pawns on the sides (or flanks) of your chess army. Why? Because then your opponent can attack the flank and you won't be able to defend it properly.

This is what happens in the shortest game of chess. It's called 'Fool's Mate' and you'll soon see how it got that name.

1

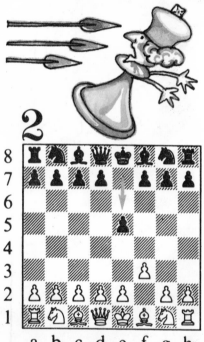

White moves a Pawn on the right flank (Kingside) of the army. Not a good move. See how the King is exposed along the diagonal!

2

Black has been much cleverer than White, by moving a centre Pawn. The black King is not exposed, but the black Queen and Bishop can get out!

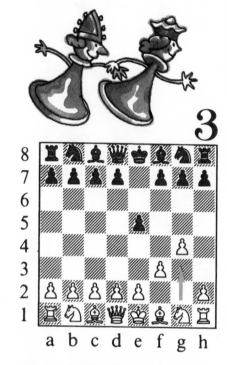

3

Oh dear! White has done it again! Moving this second Pawn makes White's Kingside even weaker than before.

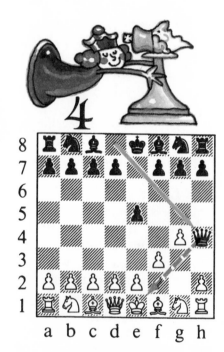

4

Out comes the black Queen—and traps the white King! That's checkmate in only two moves, because the white King cannot escape.

The Persian King's Clever Minister

The famous Persian poet Firdausi wrote a history-poem about how the Persians learned to play chess.

Firdausi told how ambassadors from the King of Hind (India) arrived at the court of the Persian King Khosrau, who ruled in the sixth century AD. The ambassadors brought with them a chessboard and pieces. They demanded that Khosrau solve the secret of the game. If he could not, then he would have to pay the King of Hind a large sum of money.

King Khosrau asked for a week to discover the secret. Days passed and many wise and clever men struggled with the game, but all failed to understand it.

Khosrau was getting very worried, and he was angry too. After all, what were wise men for if not to solve difficult problems?

The week was almost up when Khosrau's Chief Minister decided to have a try. He took the chessboard and pieces, and, for a whole day and night, he worked on the problem. At last, just as dawn broke on the next day, the Chief Minister discovered how the game of chess was played.

Turning the Tables

Later, this same Chief Minister journeyed to India. He took with him a game called Nard, which he had invented. He asked the Indians to work out how to play it. The Indians failed! So, through his clever Minister, King Khosrau got his own back in the end!

Let's Play
Another Game

Use your own chessboard to play the moves in this game. It will show you some more moves in the Ruy Lopez opening. You will see how pieces get to 'good' squares—squares from which they can attack and defend.

1 e2-e4

[chess diagram showing White pawn on e4]

As you can see, White has started by moving a Pawn forward two squares. You don't have to start every game this way—you can move a Pawn forward only one square if you want to. Now White has made the first move, it's Black's turn.

1 ...   e7-e5

[chess diagram showing Black pawn on e5]

Black has also moved a Pawn forward two squares to make room for the Bishop and Queen to get out. (If you see three dots before a move this means that Black has moved).

2 ♘g1-f3

The Knight is attacking the Pawn which Black has moved.

2 ...   ♞b8-c6

Black defends the pawn by developing the Knight.

3 ♗f1-b5

The Bishop moves out to attack the Knight which is defending the Pawn.

3 ...   a7-a6

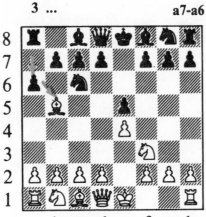

The Pawn advances to attack the Bishop. The Bishop will have to move or it will be captured by the Pawn.

4 ♗b5-a4

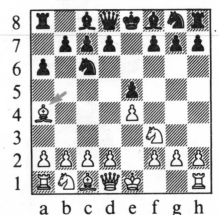

The Bishop retreats to avoid being captured.

4 ...   ♞g8-f6

Black's other Knight gets to a good square. It is attacking the white Pawn on the square e4.

5 0-0

This symbol means that White has played a special move called 'castling'. This is a move you can play in your games. The next two pages will show you how to make this move.

Castling

You ou will remember that the pieces that look like castles are called Rooks. This is because 'castles' or 'castling' in chess is a special move of the King and a Rook.

In castling the King and a Rook move together. This counts as one move. In a game, both White and Black can castle, and this is how it is done.

The King and the Rook on a1 are in their initial positions, that is the positions they occupy at the start of the game. However, the Queen, Bishop and Knight in between have all moved away to other squares on the board. Because of the gaps they have left, the King and Rook can castle, like this:

The King moves *two squares* towards the Rook, onto the square c1.

The Rook moves to the square d1.

So, when the move has been completed the two pieces end up like this:

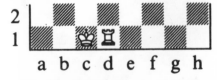

The black King can castle in the same way with a Rook on a8.

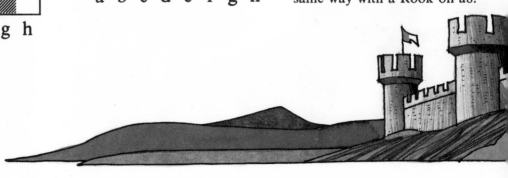

36

White can also castle using the Rook on h1. When the Bishop and Knight in between have moved away, you can then castle like this:

Again the King moves two squares towards the Rook, onto square g1. The Rook moves to the square f1. So when the move has been completed the pieces end up like this:

The black King can castle in the same way with the rook on h8.

Finishing our Game

We left our game on page 35 with White deciding to castle on the fifth move. This is how White did it.

White has started to castle by moving the King two squares towards the Rook.

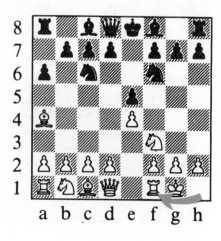

White has finished castling. The Rook has moved to the square f1. Now it is Black's turn to move again.

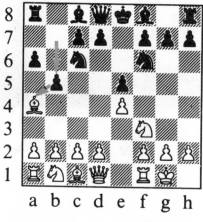

5 ...   b7-b5

The black Pawn has moved two squares to attack the white Bishop. If the Bishop captures the Pawn then it will be captured by the Pawn on a6 which is defending the attacking Pawn.

For the next few moves there will be no illustration after each White move. The illustrations will show the position after White and Black have both made one move. This will help you to practise reading the moves.

6 ♗a4-b3

White has drawn the Bishop back to safety again.

6 ...   d7-d6

Black has moved a Pawn so that it is a defender for the Pawn on e5. It has also made room for the Bishop on c8 to move into the attack later in the game.

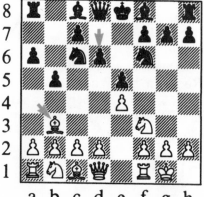

White has advanced the Knight into enemy territory! It is threatening to capture the black Pawn on f7. This is a serious threat because the white Bishop on b3 would be defending the Knight after it captured the Pawn on f7.

7 ...   d6-d5

Black has moved the Pawn to block the diagonal of the Bishop on b3. Now the Knight would not be defended if it captured the Pawn on f7 as the black King could capture it!

7 ♘f3-g5

8 e4xd5

White has made the first capture of the game! The Pawn which has made the capture is threatening to capture Black's Knight.

8 ...   ♘c6-d4

Black has moved the Knight out of danger.

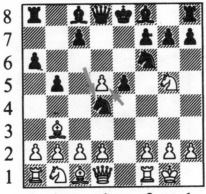

9 ♖f1-e1

White castled so that the Rook could be brought into action quickly. And now it is in action, attacking Black's Pawn on e5.

9 ...   ♗f8-c5

Black has not defended the Pawn but has brought a Bishop into an attacking position.

10 ♖e1xe5+

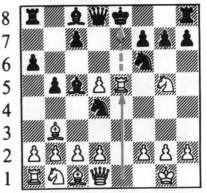

The white Rook has captured the Pawn! The '+' at the end of the move means that Black is in check! Look, the black King is now attacked by the Rook! As you know, Black will have to get the King out of check on the very next move. How will Black do that? We'll find out on page 40.

Symbols and their meanings

0-0	The King has castled with the rook on the 'h' file ('King's side').
0-0-0	The King has castled with the Rook on the 'a' file ('Queen's side').
-	A move
x	A capture
+	Check!
++	Checkmate! (sometimes just called 'mate'.)

The End of the Game

When we left the game the black King was in check. Black decided to move the King to escape from the attack by the white Rook.

10 ...   ♚e8-f8

11 h2-h3

White's Pawn move is a defending move. Now Black cannot put a piece on the square g4 because the white Pawn would be able to capture it.

11 ...   ♞f6-d7

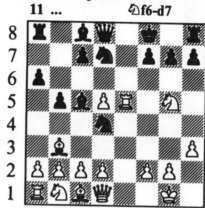

Black has moved the Knight so that it attacks the Rook on e5. Now that the Knight has moved it has opened up the diagonal so that the black Queen is attacking the white Knight on g5.

So that you can have more practice in reading notation the next diagram will appear after two moves have been played by White and by Black.

12 ♞g5xf7

White's Knight has captured a Pawn and is now attacking the black Queen *and* the black Rook.

12 ...   ♛d8-f6

Black has moved the Queen away from danger and into an attacking position. Now both the white Knight and Rook are threatened by the Queen.

13 ♞f7xh8

The white Knight has captured the Rook.

13 ...   ♞d7xe5

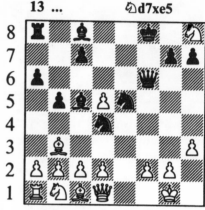

Tit for tat! The black Knight has captured the white Rook in return.

14 d2-d3

White needs to get another piece into action and makes room for the Bishop to get out.

14 ...   ♞d4xb3

The black Knight captures the Bishop which was already in play.

15 a2xb3

White recaptures the Knight. It's a fair exchange—both Bishop and Knight are worth 3 points each.

15 ...   ♛f6xf2+

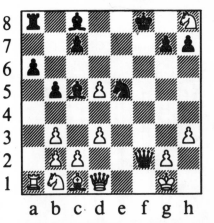

The black Queen is attacking the white King at close quarters, after capturing the Pawn on f2. It is check! The King cannot capture the Queen because she is supported by the Bishop on c5.

16 ♔g1-h2

White had to get the King out of check and has moved it away from the attack by the Queen.

16 ...   ♝c8-g4

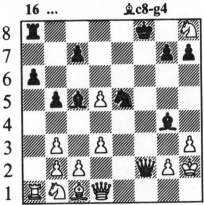

Black brought out the other Bishop to attack the white Queen. If the Queen captures the Bishop then the Knight on e5 will capture the white Queen. Queen for Bishop is not a good exchange for White (a Queen = 9 points, a Bishop = 3 points).

17 ♛d1-h1

White has moved the Queen to safety in the corner.

17 ...   ♞e5-f3++

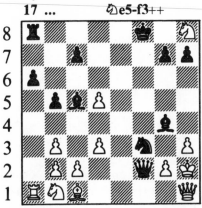

The black Knight has moved to give check to the white King. The Pawn on g2 cannot capture the Knight because then the King would be in check from the black Queen. The King cannot move to g1 or to g3 because on those squares he would again be in check, also from the black Queen. There is no escape! The game is over! It is checkmate!

41

Chess on Stamps

Many countries have shown chess pieces or chess games on their stamps. These stamps are called 'commemoratives' because they commemorate or remember important events.

In 1980, for instance, the South American country of Paraguay commemorated the world chess tournament in Mexico with nine colourful stamps. These stamps used pictures of men and women playing chess in medieval times. The pictures came from an old Spanish book about chess. Some of the players are Kings. One King is shown seated on his throne with a robe that looks like a red-and-white-checked chessboard.

In 1976, Great Britain issued a chess stamp without really meaning to! The stamp commemorated the start of book printing in Britain 500 years before, by William Caxton. One of these Caxton stamps, an 11-pence stamp marked 'William Caxton 1476' showed the printer with one of his first books. This was a book about chess called *The Game and Playe of Chesse*. It was written by a Dominican friar in the 13th century, and was one of the earliest chess books.

In 1980, the South American country of Brazil issued this stamp showing part of a chessboard. Can you tell what the chess pieces are? Look at the algebraic notation along the bottom and up the right hand side.

Another European country, Bulgaria, issued an interesting chess stamp in 1958. It showed two chessmen, as chess pieces are often called—a Knight and a King. The stamp also showed

an unusual chessboard: it was shaped like a globe. The stamp commemorated the 5th Students' World Chess Championships held in Sofia, the Bulgarian capital city.

The Caribbean island country of Cuba issued stamps for the 17th World Olympiad of Chess in 1966. The stamps show a Pawn, Knight and Rook.

Chess Computers

There were no chess-playing machines until electronic computers were invented. And there were no electronic computers until the Second World War (1939-45), when a huge computer called, appropriately, Colossus, was used to decode secret messages sent by spies and government agents. Colossus was built and used in Britain and several of the scientists who worked on it were brilliant chess players. After the war ended, some of them began working to develop a computer which could play chess.

An important breakthrough came when the stored computer program was invented in the late 1940s. A problem could be stored on coded punched tape and the tape fed into the computer which then solved the problem.

Early Computer Games
The first computers which could store chess problems were rather crude. They could not play an entire game. One chess program played at Los Alamos in the United States in 1956 used a board with only 36 squares on it, no Bishops and only six Pawns each for White and Black. It was 1960 before computers were able to cope with a board of 64 squares, although they weren't very good, and it was fairly easy to beat them. However, during the 1960s, more and more complicated chess programs were written until, eventually, the chess-playing computer became a

really tough opponent for all but the very best chess players.

World Championships
By 1974 there were enough chess computers to hold a World Computer Championship, and the first such competition was held in Stockholm, Sweden. A second Championship took place at Toronto, Canada, in 1977.

Modern Chess Computers
Today, there are many chess machines available—the Chess Challengers, Chess Traveller, Boris, Chess Champion or Chess Partner—and chess games which you can play on your own television. All of them can play chess on several levels of difficulty: the longer the machine takes to make its moves, the greater the level of difficulty. Some machines signal their moves by lighting up the figures and numbers; some can even talk! Others are 'sensory' chess computers which pick up signals from the squares when you make your own move and then light up tiny bulbs in the squares which

The Phantom chess-playing computer was programmed by Chess Master David Levy. It operates at 12 different levels, from absolute beginners to the most advanced players. The Phantom can move its own pieces by using magnets under the board. It will replay a game from start to finish so that the player can analyse his moves and see how he could have improved. Phantom obeys all the rules of chess. It will never make an illegal move nor allow the player to do so.

indicate the machine's answering move.

Some computers have been programmed with over three million different chessboard positions. They know all about the commonly used chess openings and they also know the special moves—castling, en passant, queening the pawns, etc. They won't let you cheat, either! If you make an illegal move, the machine will light up with question marks in its windows, or in some other way show that it won't accept your move.

More about Castling

Castling the King was a move invented in Spain in the 16th century. The famous player, Ruy Lopez de Sigura, wrote about it in his *Book of the Liberal Invention and Art of Chess Playing*.

Castling is a very useful move, but you can only castle at certain times.

1. You can castle only *once* in a game.
2. If you have already moved the King from its initial or starting position, you can't castle at all.
3. If you have already moved a Rook, you cannot castle with that Rook.
4. And, of course, you can't castle until the other pieces in the first rank have moved out of the way.

Castling is Forbidden!

Let's suppose you haven't already moved the King or the Rooks in the game. You *still* can't castle when this happens:

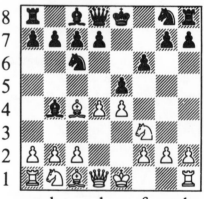

The black Bishop has the white King in check. The King cannot castle to get out of check. If the King can escape from check without moving (the other ways are blocking and capturing) then he may be able to castle later on.

Here's another situation where castling is not permitted:

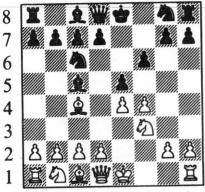

White cannot castle on the King's side, because then the King will move to square g1 and so put itself in check from the black Bishop.

The King must never make a move, castling or any other, which puts it in check.

Look Again!

Everything *looks* all right for the white King to castle here. But look more closely:

If White castled on the King's side here, the King would have to move *over* the square f1 and that square is controlled by the black Bishop. However, he can castle on the Queen's side as the King does not pass over a square where he would be in check.

Note that Black cannot castle at all in this position. Can you see why?

Answer: Because the King has already moved from his starting square at e8.

Here's a Tip for You

Because the King cannot castle if already moved from its starting position, why not force your opponent's King to move *before* it has a chance to castle. If you can do this, your opponent's King cannot take advantage of the extra protection which castling provides.

More about Chess Openings

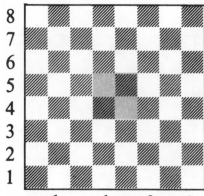

The four squares, e4, e5, d4, d5, are very important in chess. These are the squares at the centre of the battlefield where the fiercest fighting usually takes place.

Look at this diagram. It is the position after Black's 13th move in the last game you played on page 40.

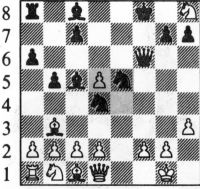

See the black Knights on the central squares e5 and d4. You'll also see that the black Bishop on c5 is very near those important centre squares. Black won that game in just four moves because of these men in the centre. Do you remember that one Knight moved to the Queen's side to capture a white Bishop? Later on the other Knight moved to the King's side to deliver checkmate.

That is why the centre is important. Pieces in the centre can move to attack and defend on both sides of the board.

Look at this diagram which shows the final position of the game on page 41. The white King has been checkmated.

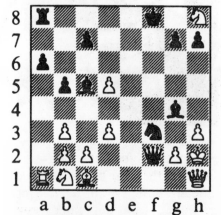

Working Together

One of the reasons that White lost the game was that none of the pieces on the Queen's side took part in the game. Half of the army was left at home! Look at the Rook on a1, the Knight on b1 and the Bishop on c1. These pieces are all on the squares where they started the game. They were unable to defend the King on the other side of the board when he needed help.

If you want to win games you must get all of your army into battle, so that they can work together to attack or defend.

The Centre of the Battlefield

So where should you put your pieces at the start of the game so that they can help to attack or defend? In the 'opening' (the chess name for the first part of the game) you should place your pieces, especially your Knights and Bishops, so that they are ready to move onto or near the four squares in the middle of the board.

The Four Knights' Opening

In the opening there are many ways of developing your pieces near to the centre. You have already seen the first few moves which have been given the name 'Ruy Lopez'. Here is another example where the first two moves by White and by Black are the same as the Ruy Lopez and then different moves are played.

1	e2-e4	e7-e5
2	♘g1-f3	♘b8-c6
3	♘b1-c3	♘g8-f6

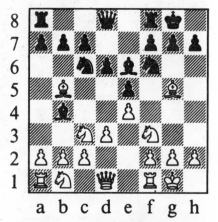

This is called the 'Four Knights' opening because all four Knights have been brought straight into the game on good squares—squares from which they can move to the centre squares in one go. But they can't

move there yet because the enemy men would capture them!

4	♗f1-b5	♗f8-b4
5	0-0	0-0

Both players have castled as soon as they could.

6	d2-d3	d7-d6
7	♗c1-g5	♗c8-e6

Now all the Bishops and Knights have been 'developed' to good squares near the centre. It is now time to think about a plan of attack. White might start to attack by playing d3-d4 threatening Black's centre pawn on e5. Try playing on from this position with a friend. Make use of your Queen and Rooks.

The Eight Golden Rules of Chess Openings

1. If you are White, always start by moving your Pawn from e2 to e4.
2. If you are Black move your e-Pawn two squares unless White plays d2-d4, in which case move your d-Pawn two squares.
3. Do not move more than two or three Pawns at the start of the game.
4. Bring out your Knights and Bishops as early as possible.
5. Castle as soon as you can.
6. Don't move your Queen until you have castled.
7. Don't move the same piece twice at the start of the game.
8. **Do not start to carry out an attack until you have carried out the first five rules!**

Laying Traps

Along column of soldiers, with their commander riding at their head, is moving along a narrow path through a forest. Everything seems quiet, just a few birds singing in the branches, perhaps a small animal rustling a leaf or two as it scuttles through the undergrowth. Then, suddenly, without warning, loud battle cries ring out among the trees. Soldiers leap from behind the tree trunks and bushes, wielding swords and daggers. The column of soldiers is surrounded. Their commander is pulled from his horse and crashes to the ground. All at once, the forest is loud with the clash and cries of battle.

It's an ambush! The enemy has sprung a trap, and anyone who escapes will be very lucky!

An ambush or suprise trap catches an enemy off guard, and even if they're going to get out of it, they are certain to suffer losses. It's not suprising then that chess, the war game, has its ambushes and traps—and they have rather painful names too: *forks, skewers* and *pins.*

The Fork

A fork, of course, has more than one prong. So has a fork in chess, as you can see here:

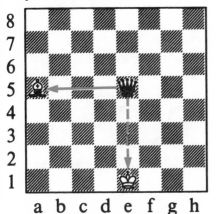

Here, the black Queen has the King in check along the e-file. At the same time, the Queen threatens the white Bishop along the fifth rank.

The white King must get out of check. The white Bishop cannot help by moving in front of it. So, the white King moves and the Queen captures the Bishop.

So you see that a fork is a trap which threatens more than one piece at a time.

The Most Dangerous Fork of All!

Here's another fork—the most dangerous one in chess, because it means the loss of the Queen.

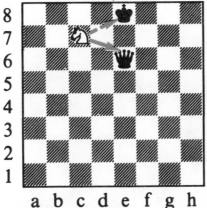

Here, the Knight has the black King in check. It also threatens the black Queen. The black King *must* move out of check, so the Knight captures the Queen.

Any two pieces can be 'forked' by one enemy piece, not just the King and one other. When two ordinary pieces are forked, usually only one manages to escape.

Skewers and Pins

The Skewer

A skewer is a way of capturing one enemy piece by threatening another, more valuable piece in front of it. Once the more valuable piece moves out of danger, the piece behind can be captured. This is called a skewer because one piece is attacked *through* another piece.

Here's a skewer in which a white Rook threatens the black Rook by giving check to the black King.

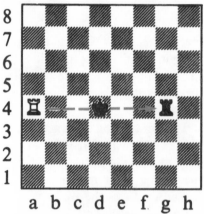

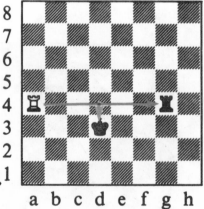

Black must move the King; then the Rook is lost.

Queens and Bishops can also skewer enemy men.

The Pin

The trap called a pin works the opposite way to a skewer. In a pin, the piece really being threatened is behind a less valuable piece in front, like this:

In this diagram the white Queen cannot move off the file because this would put the white King in check. The Queen is said to be 'pinned against' the King. Any piece may be pinned against another piece of higher value. This example is particularly dangerous because on his next move Black is going to capture the white Queen.

In this diagram White can take advantage of a pin to win the black Bishop. Can you see how?

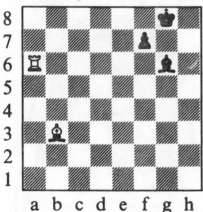

Answer: ♖a6xg6+. The Rook can capture the Bishop without fear of being recaptured by the black Pawn, which is pinned by the white Bishop on b3.

Combined Traps

Sometimes the tricks you have learned—fork, skewer and pin—can be used together with great effect. In the next position how can White use a pin and a fork to win the black Queen?

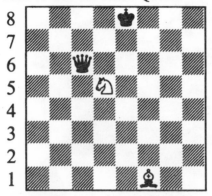

Answer: First of all White plays ♗f1-b5 which pins the black Queen to the King. In order to save the Queen Black must play ♕c6xb5. Now White has lost the Bishop but can follow up with a deadly fork: ♘d5-c7+. The King is in check and must move out of it at once.

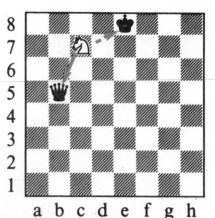

After the black King has moved, White can play ♘c7xb5 to win the black Queen.

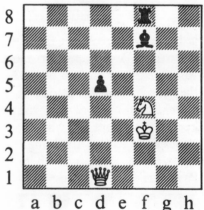

Here Black can use a pin and skewer to win the white Queen. Can you see how?

Answer: ♗f7-h5+ skewers the white King and Queen. White would like to escape from check by capturing the black Bishop with the Knight, but the Knight is pinned by the black Rook. The Knight cannot move at all! So the white King must move to escape from check and the Bishop can then capture the white Queen.

51

Dangerous Patterns in Chess

Chess players some-
times make the
mistake of thinking
that Pawns aren't
very important. This
is quite wrong. Apart from the
fact that Pawns protect more
valuable pieces on their own side,
they can be very dangerous when
attacking. So it is always wise to
keep a wary eye on what your
opponent's Pawns are doing.

Here's a situation where a
Pawn can be dangerous:

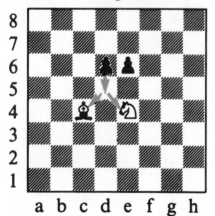

Here, the black Pawn is going to
fork. The threat is shaped like a
small triangle: after it has moved
from d6 to d5, the Pawn threatens
both the white Bishop on the left
and the white Knight on the right.
The Bishop can take the black
Pawn, but it is defended by the
Pawn on e6. So if Bishop takes
Pawn, then Pawn takes Bishop!
So either the Bishop or the Knight
must move out of danger and the
black Pawn will take the piece
that has not yet moved.

Always remember that Pawns
can move two squares forward as
a first move. The black Pawn in
our illustration was on d6. If it
was on its original square, d7,
Black would still have been able
to play d7-d5. So, watch out when
your own chess pieces are on the
fourth rank in front of you and
the enemy Pawns are on the
seventh or sixth ranks.Because of
this, try never to have two of your
pieces on the same rank with one
square between them. An enemy
pawn which is protected can
move towards them and so make
the dangerous Pawn's Triangle.

Beware the Knight's Octagon!

An octagon is an 8-sided shape like this:

A Knight on the chessboard is at the centre of an octagon. It can reach out to all the points of the octagon, because of its special way of moving.

So, when your opponent moves his Knight, look all round the points of the octagon to see where it can reach next. Your opponent may be planning to spring a fork on you, like this:

On its next move, the black Knight can take the white Pawn on f2. Now the Knight has forked the white Queen and the white Rook. The Queen will move out of danger, perhaps to e1, But then the Knight will take the Rook. The Queen can capture the black Knight, but it has lost a more important piece and a Pawn. (Rook = 5 points, Pawn = 1 point, Knight = 3 points.)

Chess Facts and Figures

DID YOU KNOW...

...that the game of chess has given the English language several expressions which are used in everyday speech?

The rank and file: means the mass of ordinary people.

Making people pawns in the game: means using unimportant people, or letting them get hurt, in order to achieve an aim.

Stalemate: means a situation where no one can win. See page 67.

Check: Is the word used to describe a sudden setback in warfare. It also means coming to a sudden halt, just as the game of chess does while the threatened King escapes from check. The word 'check' originally came from '*shah*' which is Persian, or Iranian, for 'king'. Shah mat means 'the king is dead'.

Every language has its own name for chess, of course. Here are some of them:

French	*echecs*
Spanish	*ajedrez*
German	*Schach*
Hungarian	*sakk*
Turkish	*satranc*
Russian	*shakhmati*
Swahili	*sataranji*
Iranian	*shah mat*

Look again at the Turkish word for chess, and also the Swahili, a language spoken in southeast Africa. *Satranc* (Turkish) and *sataranji* (Swahili) sound very much like *chaturanga*, the ancient Indian word for chess. Try saying the Russian word aloud.

WINNER

LOSER

Odd Chess Games

Some people play a game called **suicide chess**. The winner is the player who loses all his chess pieces first!

In another odd game, called **scotch chess**, White moves once, then Black moves twice, White moves three times and so on. If players put their opponent's King in check before they have used all their series of moves, then their turn ends.

Was This the First Chess Machine?

In 1769, nearly two centuries before our own electronic chess computers were made, a Hungarian called Wolfgang Kempelen invented a machine which played chess. Or at least, Kempelen *said* it could. It was called 'The Turk' because it had a model of a Turk in a turban sitting behind the chessboard. The board was on top of a cabinet, and there were many wires and pulleys inside.

Kempelen's machine played chess very well indeed and defeated many people who played against it. But was The Turk a genuine machine or was there a very small, but very clever real live chess player hiding inside the cabinet?

Checkmate!

As you know, the winner in a chess game is the player who checkmates the opponent's King first. The trapped King won't be able to move to safety. No other piece in his chess army will be able to rescue him—either by capturing the attacking piece or by placing itself in front of the King and so shielding him.

Here is the black King who is well and truly checkmated.

The black King cannot escape here, because he cannot stay on the rank where the Rook threatens him. His escape route on the second rank is blocked by the other white Rook on h2, which controls that rank.

Here's a checkmate by a white Queen, supported by various pieces. Set it up on your own chessboard, adding the white Bishop, Rook, Knight and King in turn.

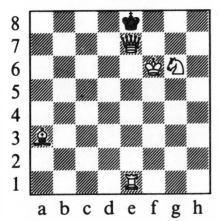

The white Queen on e7 directly threatens the black King and has him in check. The King cannot move out of danger because the white Queen controls all the available squares. Nor can the King capture the Queen, as she is protected by the white Rook, Knight, Bishop and King.

Scholar's Mate

Remember fool's mate on page 32? Here's another complete game in which one side is almost as foolish, and so loses the game. Try it out for yourself on your own chessboard. Here are the moves:

1 e2-e4   e7-e5

Both White and Black start with the same move: Pawn two squares forward.

2 ♗f1-c4

The white Bishop moves out to where it can threaten the black Pawn on f7.

2 ...   ♝f8-c5

Black has the same idea!

3 ♕d1-h5

The Bishop needs support to attack the Pawn, so White moves the Queen into position. She is threatening both the Pawn on e5 and the one on f7.

3 ...   ♞b8-c6

The black Knight protects the Pawn on e5.

4 ♕h5xf7 mate

White has closed the trap—and it's checkmate!

Where did Black go Wrong?

On the third move, ♞b8-c6.

It is *usually* a good idea to bring out your Knight early in the game, but here Black didn't see the threat to the Pawn on f7.

Put the chess pieces back to their starting positions and make the first few moves of the game again. Then, instead of Black's third move ♞b8-c6, try these moves:

a. ♛d8-e7: Protecting both the Pawn on e5 and the one on f7.

b. ♞g8-h6: Although this stops White taking the Pawn on f7 he can simply take the Pawn on e5, giving check.

Although White won this game the move ♕d1-h5 was not good because if Black had replied correctly with ♛d8-e7, the white Queen would be badly placed at the edge of the board and likely to be attacked. It is usually best not to bring your Queen into the battle until later in the game.

Further Steps to Checkmate

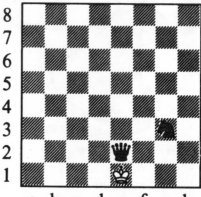

Close-up Checkmates

Naturally, the closer you get to your opponent's King, the better. This is how you can achieve 'close up' checkmate with Queen and Knight.

The white King cannot move to any of the squares on either side of him—d1 and f1, or to the squares one step up on the second rank—d2 and f2. The black Queen threatens the King on all those squares and the King cannot capture the white Queen because then he would be in check from the black Knight.

The white King would be in the same close up checkmate situation if a black Pawn were on f3 or d3. This is because the Pawn would stop the white King from capturing the black Queen.

Back Rank Mate

There are times, too, where one side contributes to its own defeat by not providing the King with an escape route. Look what's happened here:

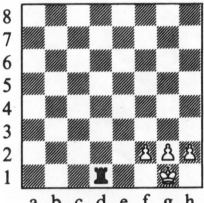

The white King castled earlier in the game, on the King's side. That's why it's on g1. But later on, the black Rook came storming down to d1 and the King has nowhere it can escape to. This is called a 'back rank' mate.

So, if you see the enemy pieces advancing down the board towards you, give your King a way out, just in case he needs it. If White had moved one of those Pawns to the third or fourth rank, the King could have escaped check that way.

Using the Rook

Suppose you were using a Rook to support the Queen and prevent it from being captured by the white King? You could place the Rook anywhere along the second rank and it would still be checkmate. However, there is also a file on the board where the Rook would achieve the same result. Can you see which one it is?

Answer: The e-file.

Using the King in Checkmate

You can use your King in some checkmates because there's a rule that Kings cannot be placed on squares next to each other. They would then have each other in check! This is how you can checkmate your opponent, using a King to support the Queen.

To escape the white Queen, the black King must move to one of three squares on the next rank—but he cannot do so! If the black King moves to d7 or e7, he would be next to the white King, and in check. If the black King moves to f7, he's still threatened by the white Queen.

Endgame Checkmates

These are the sort of positions that you are aiming for.

B

Many games of chess end up with one side having King plus Rook or Queen and the other side having a lone King. It is very important to know how to win with these pieces.

King and Queen against King

A

The plan here is to use your Queen and King to force the black King to the edge of the board as it is not possible for you to checkmate him in the middle of the board.

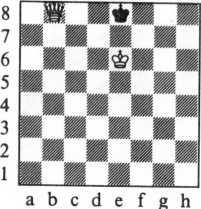

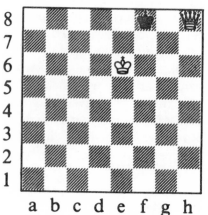

he should play:

7 ♛c6-b7   ♚d8-e8
8 ♔f5-e6   ♚e8-d8
9 ♛b7-d7 checkmate

The position is not exactly the same as in diagram B but you can see that it is checkmate! White could also have given checkmate by playing 9 ♛b7-b8.

King and Rook against King

Here again you must try to force the King to the edge of the board, place your own King opposite to stop him escaping and then give mate with your Rook, as in this position:

There are several ways of making the black King move to the edge of the board.

From diagram A White could play:

1 ♛a1-c3

This is as near to the black King as the white Queen can go without being taken.

1 ...   ♚d5-e4

The King is trying to keep in the centre of the board where he cannot be checkmated.

2 ♔h1-g2   ♚e4-d5
3 ♔g2-f3   ♚d5-d6

The black King is forced to move towards the edge of the board.

4 ♔f3-e4

Better than ♛c3-c4 when the black King can return to the centre (♚d6-e5).

4 ...   ♚d6-e6
5 ♛c3-c6+   ♚e6-e7
6 ♔e4-f5   ♚e7-d8

Now White must be careful. If he plays ♔f5-e6 then the black King cannot move without being in check and the game is a draw (stalemate—see page 67). Instead

It takes longer to force the King to the edge of the board with a Rook and King than with a Queen and King. To do it you must use the idea of 'reducing the rectangle'.

Reducing the Rectangle

In the previous position, as long as the white Rook stays on d4 the black King cannot escape from the rectangle marked on the diagram. If it is Black's move he could play ♔c5-c6 after which White would play ♖d4-d5, reducing the size of the rectangle. By repeating this process you can see how the black King will be forced into a smaller and smaller rectangle until he is at the edge of the board.

Look at diagram A again. If you replace the white Queen with a white Rook this is how the game might go:

  1 ♖a1-a4

Preventing the black King from moving to c4, d4 or e4.

1 ...	♔d5-e5
2 ♔h1-g2	♔e5-d5
3 ♔g2-f3	♔d5-e5
4 ♖a4-e4+	♔e5-d5
5 ♔f3-e3	

Now the black King is trapped inside the rectangle at the top left hand side of the board.

5 ...	♔d5-c5
6 ♖e4-d4	

Making the rectangle smaller.

6 ...	♔c5-c6
7 ♔e3-e4	♔c6-c5
8 ♔e4-e5	♔c5-c6
9 ♖d4-d5	

Once again the rectangle has been made smaller.

9 ...	♔c6-c7
10 ♖d5-d6	♔c7-c8

The size of the rectangle has been reduced once again.

11 ♔e5-d5	♔c8-c7
12 ♔d5-c5	♔c7-b7
13 ♖d6-c6	

The rectangle is getting smaller.

13 ...	♔b7-a7
14 ♖c6-b6	

Now the rectangle is just two squares.

14 ...	♔a7-a8
15 ♔c5-c6	♔a8-a7
16 ♔c6-c7	♔a7-a8
17 ♖b6-a6 mate	

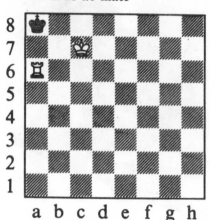

A Quicker Way to Checkmate

There are other ways of getting checkmate with King and Rook, and these are often quicker than 'reducing the rectangle'.

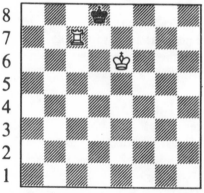

Here White does not have to reduce the rectangle by playing ♖c7-e7 etc. Instead White can use a waiting move by the Rook to give checkmate in just two moves. If the Rook retreats along the 'c' file then the black King will be forced to move to e8 and the Rook can then checkmate on c8. Try it for yourself.

1 ♖c7-c1	♔d8-e8
2 ♖c1-c8 mate	

Special Moves

Discovered check means moving one of your pieces so that another piece puts the enemy King in check. Here is a discovered check:

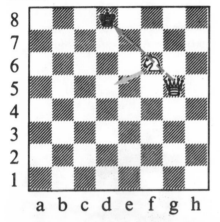

If White moves the Knight out of the way, the white Queen has the black King in check.

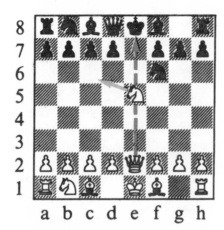

Here White can give a discovered check with the Queen by moving the Knight out of the way. If the Knight moves to c6 then the black King must get out of check with either ♛d8-e7 or ♝f8-e7. The white Knight can then take the black Queen whether it is still on d8 or has moved to e7. Because Black was going to be checked by the white Queen, the white Knight had a 'free' move which allowed him to go to c6. Other Knight moves would still have given check but would not have forced the win of the black Queen.

After ♘g5xf7+, the King must move to g8.

Discovered checks can be very dangerous because the piece that moves away has a 'free' move. Look at the next diagram.

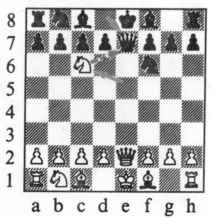

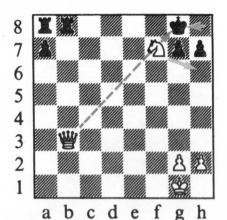

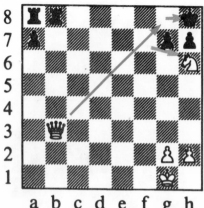

White could now move the Knight and give a discovered check, but how can the black rook be prevented from taking the Queen?

The answer is to give a double check by moving the Knight to h6. Black cannot capture the Knight and the Queen both at the same time so must move the King. Moving it to f8 lets White give checkmate by playing the Queen to f7.

To avoid this the King must go to h8. Now White has a very surprising move: ♛b3-g8 check. Black has to get out of check but cannot capture the Queen with the King because it is defended by the Knight. So the Queen must be taken by the Rook and then White can play ♘h6-f7 checkmate.

This is called a 'smothered mate' because the black King is surrounded by his own men and cannot move out of trouble.

En Passant: A Special Capture by Pawns

Pawns have a special way of capturing each other in certain circumstances. It is called capture by 'en passant', which is French for 'in passing.' An en passant capture can take place only after a Pawn has advanced two squares.

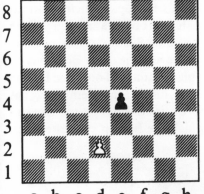

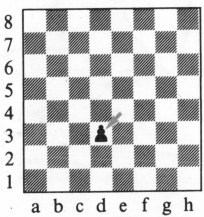

The white Pawn has made its first move—two squares forward to d4, so it's on the same rank as the black Pawn.

Players sometimes make this white Pawn move, thinking they can get the white Pawn past the black one, but they can't because...

The black Pawn can now move as if the white Pawn had moved only one square, to d3, not d4!

The black Pawn therefore captures the white one, on the diagonal, and so lands where you see the black Pawn in this third picture—on the third rank of the 'd' file. The white Pawn, of course, is removed from the board.

Black doesn't have to make this en passant capture and can choose another move instead. However, if Black does not capture the white Pawn immediately then it has escaped and may not be taken on a subsequent move.

It's a Draw!

Suppose one side has lost an entire army so that the King is alone and unprotected on the board. If the opponent still has the more powerful pieces at his command—the Queen or the Rooks—then the lone King has very little chance of escaping checkmate and defeat. It's better to resign—that is, give up.

However, in certain circumstances, a lone King can produce a drawn game. If, for instance, Black has only a King and White has a King and a Knight—then White can chase the black King all over the board—and the King will always escape from check—try it and see. It's the same if it's a black King against a white King and white Bishop. The Bishop can threaten the black King only on squares of one colour—on black *or* white, not on both.

If you look at White's or Black's Bishops in their positions at the start of a game, you will see that one Bishop is on a white square and the other Bishop is on a black square. If only one Bishop is left, all the lone enemy King has to do is to keep to the squares which the Bishop cannot reach.

Perpetual Check

Of course, the King doesn't have to be alone in order to produce a drawn game. Here's a situation that inevitably leads to a draw:

The white Queen has the black King in check along the 'a' file. To get out of check the black Queen must move to a7. The black Queen is now between the black King and the white Queen. So, White moves ♛a6-c8—and the black King is in check again from the Queen. But then the black Queen moves to b8 and is in between again, protecting the King.

The two Queens can go on swinging back and forth in this way for ever. This is called *perpetual check*.

This is a waste of time. It's best to declare a draw and start again.

Other Times to Call a Truce

Apart from perpetual check and lack of enough pieces to give checkmate, there are four other situations where the game is a draw.

1. *Repeated position* If exactly the same position is reached three times then the game is a draw. This most often happens when there is perpetual check, but it is possible to reach a situation where players repeat moves even though there is no check involved and the same position occurs three times.

2. *The fifty move rule* If fifty moves by both White and Black pass without a piece being captured or a Pawn being moved then the game is a draw. This does not happen very often but can be important when grandmasters (expert chess players) are playing chess.

3. *Stalemate* If one side is not in check but has no legal moves that can be made then the game is a draw.

In this position White has almost given checkmate, but has forgotten to leave space for the black King to move. It is Black's turn to move, but there are no squares the King can go to without being in check so the game is a draw.

4. *Truce* Both players may also, if they wish, agree to a draw at any time during a game. Grandmasters often do this when they do not think that either side will be able to win. However you are not advised to offer a draw to your opponent until you have been playing for several years and can learn to recognise a position where neither side is likely to win.

Pawn Promotion

ere's another good reason why you should never underestimate your Pawns. Pawns have a chance of glory, usually in the last stages of a game. For they can become extra Queens if they safely reach the back rank of the enemy lines. A Pawn which does this must be converted into any other piece (except the King). However, you should almost always choose the Queen which is the most powerful piece of all.

This is why this special process is sometimes called *Queening the Pawn*. Here are some of the tactics that might be used:

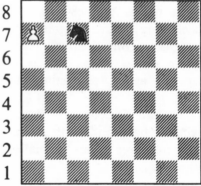

The white Pawn is heading for a8, where it can become a Queen. The black Knight is guarding the 'queening square', waiting to capture the newly made Queen.

Test Yourself

If Black wanted to use a Bishop instead of a Knight to guard the queening square, where should it be placed?

Answer:

Along the diagonal a8–h1.

68

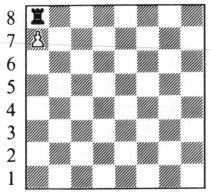

a b c d e f g h

Here, the black Rook has moved to occupy White's queening square so that the white Pawn cannot move up to it. The Rook, of course, can capture the white Pawn on its next move. However, any black piece, except another Pawn, can block the white Pawn's path to the queening square, whether or not it can capture the Pawn afterwards.

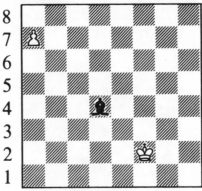

a b c d e f g h

The black Bishop has placed itself on the diagonal between the white King, which it holds in check, and the white Pawn. The King must move out of check, and the Bishop then captures the white Pawn. So there goes White's chance of queening a Pawn.

Defending Your Pawn

How can you defend a Pawn if you want to Queen it?

1. If you have a Rook make sure it is behind the Pawn or on the same rank, so that it gives protection against attack.

2. Make sure your King is not on the same diagonal, file or rank as your Pawn or an enemy piece which may do what the black Bishop has done in our illustration—check the King and trap the Pawn at the same time.

3. Always try to defend the file the Pawn moves up on, and at the same time, guard the queening square, like this:

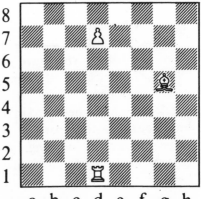

a b c d e f g h

And do move the Pawn up at every opportunity. You can *make* an opportunity by putting your opponent's King in check. Your opponent will have to deal with the check, so you can use your next move to move the Pawn up another square.

Test Your Skill in Giving

Sometimes you do not have to wait until there are only a few pieces left before you have the chance to checkmate your opponent. Very often checkmate can be delivered in the 'middlegame'—that part of the game after the opening, but before most of the pieces have been exchanged off.

Here are some positions to test your skill in giving mate. In every diagram it is White to play and give checkmate next move.

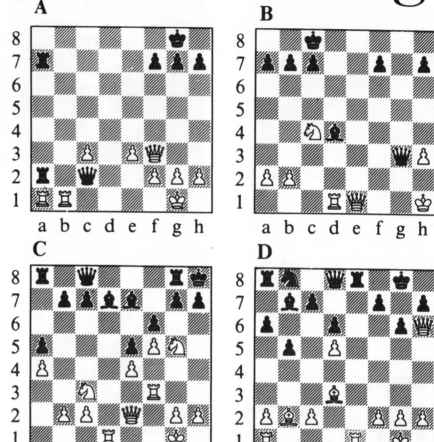

A

B

C

D

Mate

E

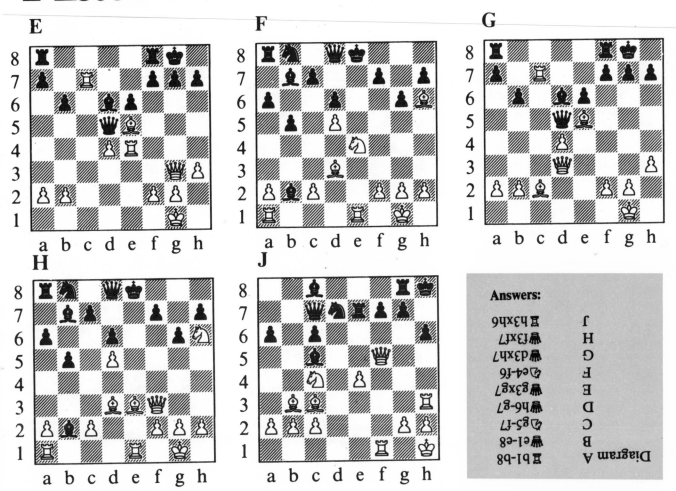

F

G

H

J

71

Exchanging Pieces

In chess, as in war, you will capture some enemy men and you will lose some of your own. In order to win you must try to gain more than you lose. On page 25 the values of the men were shown in points. Do you remember them? Here they are again:

Queen	9 points
Rook	5 points
Bishop	3 points
Knight	3 points
Pawn	1 point

Sometimes these values do not apply. A Rook which is left in the corner and never takes part in the battle may be worth no points! Giving up your Queen for a Pawn is a loss of 8 points, but if by doing it you can checkmate your opponent with another man, then it is worth it. However, the point values of the men apply to most situations which will arise on your chessboard. You can use them to decide when an exchange of men is to your advantage.

Test Yourself

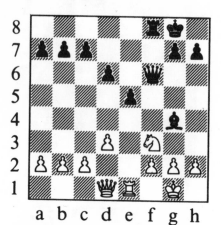

In this position it is Black to play and win points. Can you see how?

Answer:

1...♗g4xf3 2 ♕d1xf3 ♕f6xf3
3 g2xf3 ♖f8xf3

After all these moves Black has won Knight + Queen + Pawn = 13 points and White has won Bishop + Queen = 12 points, a gain of 1 point for Black. White did not have to exhange Queens and could have played 2 g2xf3 ♕f6xf3; 3 ♕d1-d2, but still ends up by losing 1 point.

Making the Right Decision

Sometimes the point values will help you to choose the best course of action. Here the black Queen is trapped in a corner and there is no escape. As the Queen is lost, Black needs to work out the best possible exchange. Can you see what it is?

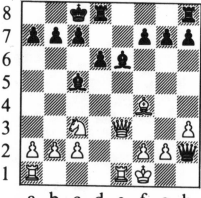

Answer:

The Queen could capture either the Pawn on h3 or the one on g2 but White would capture the Queen and gain 8 points. If the black Queen captured the white Bishop on f4 and was then captured by the white Queen, this would be a loss of 6 points. However, there is an even better exchange which loses only 4 points: **1...♕h2-h1+ 2 ♔f1-e2 ♕h1xe1+ 3 ♔e2xe1**
Given that Black had to lose the Queen, this was the best exchange.

Try Again

White to move and win points. Can you see how?

Answer:
1 ♖f2xf6 ♛d8xf6 2 ♕d1xd7
White has won a Knight and Bishop worth 6 points and lost a Rook worth 5 points, a gain of 1 point.

Chess Manners

There are various laws of chess which you must follow when playing a game. In general, you should always be courteous to your opponent—even if he or she beats you. It is usual for players to shake hands at the end of a game.

Touch and Move

There is also one particular law which you should observe when playing your games. This law says that if you touch one of your own men with the intention of moving it then you must move it if you can. The 'touch and move' law does not apply to a man which has been touched accidentily. In the same manner, if you touch one of your opponent's men then you must capture it if you can.

If you touch a man that you cannot move because it

would place your own King in check then the 'touch and move' law does not apply and you can make any other legal move.

Once you have moved a man to a new square and taken your hand off it, then you have completed your move and you cannot take it back—even if it was a very bad move! Until you have let go of the man you can still make a different move with it, but as you have already touched it you will have to make a move of some kind with it, if you can. If you want to adjust a piece which has not been placed in the middle of a square you may do so as long as you say "I adjust" to your opponent before touching it. If you fail to warn your opponent *before* you touch the piece then you will have to follow the touch and move law.

Chess Games from the Past

T his is a game played between Napoleon and a player called Remusat. Remusat, naturally, let Napoleon win: Napoleon was, after all, the conqueror of the larger part of Europe, and in 1802, when this game was played, was soon to make himself Emperor of the French.

Set up the game on your chessboard and watch how Remusat, playing White, allowed Napoleon to win:

White: Remusat	Black: Napoleon
1 e2-e4	**♞g8-f6**
Moving a Pawn into the centre and opening lines.	Developing to attack White's Pawn
2 d2-d3	**♞b8-c6**
Defending the Pawn	Bringing another piece into play
3 f2-f4	**e7-e5**
A third Pawn move!	Fighting for the centre
4 f4xe5	**♞c6xe5**
Yet another Pawn move!	Recapturing the Pawn
5 ♞b1-c3	**♞f6-g4**
At last White brings a piece into play	It's not a good idea to move the Knight again
6 d3-d4	**♛d8-h4+**
Attacking the Knight but leaving the King in danger	Taking advantage of White's Pawn moves
7 g2-g3	**♛h4-f6**
Blocking the check and attacking the Queen	Threatening to give checkmate on f2
8 ♞g1-h3	**♞e5-f3+**
Preventing the checkmate	Check!
9 ♚e1-e2	**♞f3xd4+**
The King escapes	Black has won a Pawn
10 ♚e2-d3	**♞g4-e5+**
The King chases after the Knight	Sacrificing a Knight to draw the white King into a mating net
11 ♚d3xd4	**♝f8-c5+**
The King greedily grabs the Knight	Sacrificing the Bishop to force mate in just two more moves
12 ♚d4xc5	**♛f6-b6+**
The King gobbles up another piece	Forcing the King to a square where he can be mated
13 ♚c4-d5	**♛b6-d6 mate**
There is no other move	Checkmate!

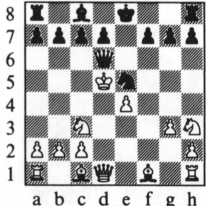

Remusat made his first deliberate mistake with his third move, f2-f4. As in fool's mate (see page 32) this exposes the white King to attack along the diagonal e1-h4. Remusat next allowed Napoleon's Knights to put his King in check, one after the other, and then moved his King out into the centre of the board without any protection at all. No wonder Remusat lost—he intended to. He gave a very good demonstration of how *not* to play winning chess!

A BRILLIANT GAME

Now that you have seen how not to play chess, here is a game by a brilliant player.

In 1858, the American chess master Paul Morphy won this game against two European noblemen, the Duke of Brunswick and Count Isouard. At the time, all three were attending an opera performance in Paris and they played chess during the interval. Here are the moves for you to play on your own chessboard:

White: Morphy	Black: Brunswick and Isouard
1 e2-e4	e7-e5
Opening lines	Black does the same
2 ♘g1-f3	d7-d6
Developing to attack the Pawn	Defending the Pawn
3 d2-d4	♗c8-g4
Attacking the Pawn again	A pin!
4 d4xe5	♗g4xf3
Capturing a Pawn	To stop White winning a Pawn by 3...d6xe5 4♛d1xd8+ ♚e8xd8 5 ♘f3xe5
5 ♛d1xf3	d6xe5
To regain the piece by developing one	To regain the Pawn
6 ♗f1-c4	♘g8-f6
Threatening checkmate by ♛f3xf7	Blocking the 'f' file
7 ♛f3-b3	♛d8-e7
A fork! White threatens to capture the Pawn on f7 with the Bishop and the Pawn on b7 with the Queen	Defending the Pawn nearest the King
8 ♘b1-c3	c7-c6
The Queen could have captured the Pawn on b7 but White prefers to get another piece into play before sending the Queen down the board	This Pawn moves so that the Queen is defending the Pawn on b7
9 ♗c1-g5	...

Another pin

At this stage, halfway through the game, the chessboard looks like this:

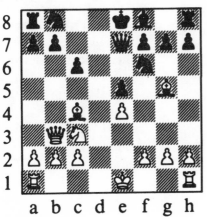

9 ...	b7-b5

Trying to force the Bishop to retreat

10 ♘c3xb5	c6xb5

A sacrifice! White gets only two Pawns for the Knight—a loss of one point— but will be able to attack the black King with every piece!

Otherwise Black would just lose a Pawn

11 ♗c4xb5+	♘b8-d7

Now the black King is in danger

Developing a piece to get the King out of check

12 0-0-0	♖a8-d8

White has castled on the Queen's side (0-0-0). This brings the white Rook to square d1, where it can join in the attack on the black King, and exert pressure against the black Knight pinned by the Bishop on b5.

Defending the Knight

13 ♖d1xd7	♖d8xd7

Another sacrifice. Black must recapture with the Rook or lose material

Now the Rook is pinned by the Bishop on b5

14 ♖h1-d1	♛e7-e6

White's last piece joins in the attack

Freeing the Knight on f6 which was pinned by the Bishop on g5

Now the black and white Rooks threaten each other, and so do the black and white Queens. Next, though, the white Bishop captures the black Rook to put the King in check

15 ♗b5xd7+	15 ♘f6xd7

The black Knight captures the white Bishop, but this move allows the other white Bishop to control the diagonal from h4-d8. Watch that remaining white Bishop carefully.

Next, White sacrifices the Queen, but the sacrifice has a clever purpose

16 ♛b3-b8+	♘d7xb8

The black Knight *must* capture the white Queen to get the black King out of check, for the King cannot move. Can you see why?
Answer: The black King would be in check from the white Bishop on g5.

Next, White moves 17 ♖d1-d8—and it's checkmate!

By forcing the black Knight to move from d7, White can move his Rook all the way up the d-file to checkmate the black King on square d8. The checkmating square is, of course, guarded by the white Bishop.

Chess Terms

Capture: Landing on a square occupied by an opponent's chess piece and then removing it from the board.

Castling: Crossing over the positions of the King and Rook on the first rank after the intervening pieces have moved away.

Check: When a King is threatened by an opponent's piece and must then escape before any other move can be made.

Checkmate: The end of a game. In checkmate, the King is in check and cannot escape, either by moving to another square or by placing another piece between himself and the attacking opponent, or by capturing the opponent.

Development: In the first part of the game, moving up pieces from the first and second ranks to take part in the battle in the centre of the board.

Diagonal: A row of black squares or white squares which slant across the chessboard touching from corner to corner.

Draw: Neither side has won the game.

End Game: The last moves in a game, when both sides have lost most of their pieces.

En passant: A special capture for pawns only (see page 65).

File: A row of black and white squares running from the top to the bottom of the chessboard. There are eight of them.

Fork: A trap in chess (see page 49).

Gambit: Deliberately letting a pawn or piece be captured in the opening, in order to gain an advantage later on.

Grandmaster: An expert chess player.

King's Side: For White, the King's side is the right hand side of the board. For Black, it is the left hand side.

Mate: Same as Checkmate.

Opening: The first nine or ten moves of a game, when both players are moving their pieces into the centre of the board.

Pin: A trap (see page 51).

Promotion: When a Pawn reaches the opponent's back rank and becomes a Queen, Rook, Bishop or Knight.

Queen's Side: For White, the Queen's side is the left hand side of the board. For Black, it is the right hand side.

Rank: A row of black and white squares which runs from one side to the other side of the board. There are eight of them.

Skewer: A trap in chess (see page 50).

Stalemate: When the side to move is not in check but cannot move at all without putting the King in check from an opposing piece.

Chess Notation

The moves in the games in this book have been written down in figurine algebraic notation, but this is not the only way of writing down moves.

In another form of algebraic notation, capital letters are used instead of pictures (figurines) to show which piece is moved. This is a notation you can use to write down the moves played in your own games. The letters used are: K-King Q-Queen R-Rook B-Bishop N-Knight. These are the initial letters of of the pieces except for the Knight which has the same initial letter as the King. To avoid confusion, 'N' is used for the Knight.

The Pawn doesn't have a special letter. To write down a Pawn move you just give the squares that are involved.

This is how the moves of scholar's mate on page 57 are written down in ordinary algebraic notation:

```
1  e2-e4       e7-e5
2  Bf1-c4      Bf8-c5
3  Qd1-h5      Nb8-c6
4  Qh5xf7 + +
```

When you get used to algebraic notation you will be able to use the shortened form which leaves out the squares of departure (the first square). Written in shortened form the moves of scholar's mate (above) would appear as: 1 e4 e5 2 Bc4 Bc5 3 Qh5 Nc6 4 Qxf7 + +